Copyright © 2016 Andrea Chat

The rights of Andrea Chatten to be identified as the author of this work have been asserted in accordance with the Copyright, Designs and Patents Act 1988.
All rights reserved.

First published in 2016 by
The Solopreneur Publishing Company Ltd
Cedars Business Centre, Barnsley Road, Hemsworth, West Yorkshire WF9 4PU
www.thesolopreneur.co.uk

The publisher makes no representation, expressed or implied, with regards to the accuracy of the information contained in this book, and cannot accept any responsibility or liability.

Except for the quotation of small passages for the purposes of criticism and review, no part of this publication may be reproduced, stored in a retrieval system, or transmitted, in any form or by any means, electronic, mechanical, photocopying, recording or otherwise, except under the terms of the Copyright, Designs and Patents Act 1988 without the prior consent of the publisher at the address above.
Printed in the UK

For further copies, please go online to www.theblinks.co.uk and Amazon. Also available on Kindle.

# Dedication

To you for being a children's champion - committed and dedicated to developing happiness and well-being.

**Andrea Chatten**  Msc, MBPsS, PGCL&M, Bed(Hons), Dip.CBT

Andrea has been a specialised teacher for over 25 years, working with children from ages 5-16 with emotional and behavioural difficulties. She is currently Director and 'Lead Children's Emotional & Behavioural Psychologist' at Unravel CEBPC Ltd with schools and families in and around Sheffield and across the UK.

Developing positive, trusting relationships has always been at the heart of her practice with children and young people to nudge them into improved psychological well-being. Over the years, Andrea has developed and applied many positive developmental psychology approaches.

This insight is incorporated into her stories, in order to help children, young people and their families to gain more understanding and potential strategies to try to deal with a range of behavioural issues which children and young people could experience.

Andrea created 'The Blinks' so that parents could also benefit from reading the books with their children, especially if they identify with the children in the stories and their family circumstances. Both parent and child can learn how to manage early forms of psychological distress as a natural part of growing up, rather than it become problematic when not addressed in its early stages.

'The Blinks' is a series of books which discreetly apply lots of psychological theory throughout the stories, including Cognitive Behavioural Therapy, Developmental and Positive Psychology approaches.

This, book 3 in the series, aims to help children understand self-esteem and the importance of liking who we are, fundamental to positive well-being.

Book 1 in the series tackles the issue of worry and how to prevent this everyday cognition from becoming a more serious anxiety in the future. Book 2 – Anger helps children understand the physiological aspects of anger, what can trigger it and most importantly, how to control it.

## Introduction

The Blinks' books have been created to help children, young people and their families understand the feelings that can underpin emotional and behavioural issues. With greater insight into emotions, the strategies and techniques provided in this book can help manage and change the intensity and duration of problematic behaviours over time.

The third Blinks' book 'Self-esteem' shares the story of twins Bladen and Tim who have spent many years being unkind to each other. This has not helped them develop very positive feelings about themselves. This low self-esteem has affected their confidence, friendships, who they believe they are, and their happiness.

Positive self-esteem is the ability to like ourselves and accept our faults. We are all flawed. No-one is perfect. Yet many of us spend too much time and attention focussing on our weaknesses, imperfections and failings, rather than on what makes us unique and brilliant for who we are.

It also involves taking responsibility for our choices and addressing them with honesty, so as not to lay blame elsewhere. In order to develop and grow, we need to have the courage to learn as much as we can from situations, our choices and actions so that we hold onto our personal power. By blaming someone or something else, we are not learning from our actions and what we could do differently next time.

Our self-esteem dictates what we think and feel about ourselves and this fundamentally feeds into how we behave, interact with others and generally how confidently we apply and motivate ourselves. In this story, Bladen and Tim's low self-worth creates many problems in their lives. It impacts first and foremost on the misunderstanding of who they believe they are, which activates many sensitivities towards each other. This sibling rivalry, amongst other things, becomes intolerable and causes many difficulties for the family as a whole.

As with all The Blinks' books, help is on hand and Larry Love-Who-You-Are works closely with the twins and the family to help them make positive changes. Our self-esteem is not set in stone. We can change how we feel by changing what we think and changing what we do. It is important to remember this crucial formula of understanding/insight + action which lays down the foundations for positive change and improved well-being.

| **Understanding/ insight** | + | **Strategies/ effort/action** | = | **Success/positive change/ happier children and young people** |
|---|---|---|---|---|

This book aims to help you as the active adult in a child or young person's life, to understand the theory behind The Blinks' interventions, used to support Bladen and Tim with their low self-esteem. The more empowered you are about your understanding of difficult feelings, the more confident you will be to guide and nudge the children and young people in your care towards improved emotional understanding and self-management.

## Section 1 - The Psychology of Self-esteem.

Until recently young children, pre-schoolers, were always thought to be too young to have a strong sense of their overall positive or negative sense of self. However, recent research suggests that a child's sense of self-esteem is evident much earlier than previously thought. Although these findings contradict the notion that self-esteem develops over childhood, it is still important to recognise that how much we like and value ourselves is affected by the experiences and affirmations we encounter across the lifespan. Self-esteem is not fixed and modifications can happen at any age.

When children do not receive positive recognition, attention and appreciation during childhood, their self-esteem is hindered. Children are highly sensitive to the messages communicated to them by our actions. Too often we forget the more subtle messages we are sending out to children and young people. Small rejections over time can contribute to what a child thinks about themselves. Actions that can diminish a child's self-esteem include:

1. Not meeting a child's basic needs.
2. Being over-protective.
3. Being sarcastic when answering a question.
4. Scowling when we are looking at a test result.
5. Labelling a child negatively.
6. Not providing an explanation. Children need 'Whys'.
7. Harsh punishments.
8. Being exposed to or being forced to do age inappropriate things

9. Ignoring or denying a child's feelings.
10. Ridiculing, putting down or humiliating a child.
11. Comparing a child unfavourably to other people.
12. Allowing access to unrealistic ideas presented by the media.
13. Providing inconsistent approaches to behaviour.
14. Violence against a child, threatened or actual, verbal or physical.

Every now and then we may feel disappointed or frustrated with our children, this is normal. However if most or our actions are unkind, unloving and resentful, then this will impact negatively on how our children perceive themselves and on how loveable they feel they are. Poor self-esteem will then develop over time.

Poor self-esteem presents as:
- a negative view of self
- little awareness of personal needs or strengths
- feelings of worthlessness
- poor ability to be objective in negative situations
- taking things personally and feeling that everything is their fault

This leads to:
- low self-confidence
- difficulties in expressing wants, needs and ideas
- fear of failure
- nervousness when faced with new challenges
- finding it difficult to cope when things go wrong

Children then develop:
- lower self-esteem
- a sense that people don't like them
- a perception that no-one really cares or respects their feelings

- ☹ reduced beliefs about their capabilities
- ☹ weaker relationships
- ☹ passive, aggressive or manipulative behaviours
- ☹ social withdrawal

Positive self-esteem is fostered from warm, supportive relationships which allow children to feel loved. This external love becomes locked away inside our children and provides them with a sense of value and worth. These affirmations develop their own blank canvas which represents the image of who they feel they are.

As parents, carers and teachers we are fundamental in how our child's canvas develops. How much colour is present? How much grey? How the colours are dispersed, how bright those colours are and more importantly how appealing the final product is regarded highly within our culture.

Raising children with good self-esteem takes huge, regular bundles of patience. Children translate that patience into love. Patience means being gentle. Patience makes us listen more actively. Patience means we find time in this crazy fast world to stop and just be in the moment with our children. This love then becomes locked away inside children and activates a core message that runs through them like a stick of rock.
In order for children to develop a good level of self-esteem, the message needs to be positive - *"I am okay. I'm not perfect, I have faults, but I am okay. I am worthy of love."* Reading this may make you feel pressured as parenting is your job, but every human being makes mistakes. You too just need to be okay, not perfect; you too have flaws and bad days. I had to have a serious word with myself when both my children were small; coping day to day with sleep deprivation, a hungry breastfeeding baby and a toddler was tough. Some days I was not the best mum. My career experiences meant that I had only ever worked with children with emotional and behavioural difficulties, it seemed so easy to mess up children and damage their self-esteem. Please let me reassure you now - it isn't that easy.

Long term damage to self-esteem develops over time, not from a bad day here and there. It is how we re-engage with our child afterwards that is essential. Apologies and explanations mean we take responsibility for our negative actions and don't leave them with the child. It also means that we model real emotions and make mistakes - a normal part of being human. If we don't re-connect emotionally afterwards, that can make a child feel like it is their fault and they aren't good enough. It is this internal dialogue that can also begin the spiral of low self-esteem.

Children's self-esteem starts with us. We have to find as many ways to show children that we not only love them but like them. Also, it is essential that if our children have pushed us into going off them, that this stage is only ever temporary and we the parents, carers or teachers, get back on them as soon as possible. Children are highly sensitive to this emotional withdrawal and that too fosters low self-esteem.

Raising children with good self-esteem is not difficult if we practise positive parenting and keep reflecting throughout the process. None of us are perfect but with love, patience, and emotional warmth our children's canvases can be bright, colourful and most of all, happy.

Positive self-esteem is associated with:
- ☺ a strong sense of self
- ☺ gender identity
- ☺ an ability to learn from negative experiences
- ☺ recognition and willingness to work at our weaknesses

In turn this leads to:
- ☺ good self-confidence
- ☺ development of honest, direct and respectful relationships
- ☺ making positive choices

☺ embracing new challenges

☺ bouncing back after setbacks or failures with reduced devastation

From this children develop:

☺ enhanced self-esteem

☺ perceptions that people respect and care for them

☺ a strong self-image

☺ a sense of worth and self-respect

☺ greater self-confidence

☺ good relationships

☺ happiness and security about life

☺ increased resilience

**Top tips for supporting low self-esteem**

- Let your eyes 'light up' as often as possible when you engage with children and young people
- Keep an open dialogue from as young as possible. Create opportunities for children to express emotions and talking about issues as a normal part of life
- Enjoy unconditional time together. It isn't the amount of time that you spend with your children, it is the quality of that time
- Provide your children with as many enriching experiences as possible. They don't know what they are capable of until they try
- Make eating well, exercise, relaxation and sleep important routines. It is difficult to feel good about ourselves if we are tense, unfit and tired
- Set achievable goals
- Help children practise seeing themselves doing well in a task, or act as if they felt that they have that new level of confidence. Remember fake it till you make it!

### ***Activities and questions for discussion with children and young people***

1. Have you ever felt like Bladen and Tim? When?
2. Do you think that you are never going to make mistakes? Why?
3. Would you like to think that you could never make the same mistake twice? How could you do this?
4. What do you say to yourself when something goes wrong or you make a mistake?
5. Do you know what it means to forgive yourself?
6. What could you say to yourself in the future when you get something wrong or make a mistake?
7. Try keeping a diary of things that make you feel good, that put a smile on your face or were random acts of kindness. Try to increase the number of things each week.
8. Practise giving yourself positive messages. Instead of saying:

    *"I've never done this before. I am going to get it wrong and show myself up in front of everyone."*

    Say:

    *"I've never done this before. It will be fun and I will learn something new."*

    Try changing round some of your other negative messages.

## Section 2 – Cognitive Behavioural Therapy (CBT) approaches to support self-esteem

CBT is a psychological intervention that helps us recognise how thoughts affect our feelings, and fundamentally what we believe about ourselves and our world. The principles of CBT are based on two main factors:
1. If we think something for long enough, we will eventually feel it.
2. The longer we feel it, the more likely we are to believe it.

Bladen and Tim are pre-occupied with negative thinking about themselves throughout the story which understandably creates feelings of low self-esteem. Before Larry Love-Who-You-Are became involved, the twins' low self-worth was having an impact on their friendships, abilities and general well-being. They didn't have the knowledge or tools to try to reduce these difficult feelings. With the help of Larry Love-Who-You-Are Bladen, Tim and their parents learn how to face some very personal challenges and, more importantly, learn to like who they are.

### *Thoughts are just guesses!*

An essential part of CBT and positive psychology is understanding how our thoughts underpin and impact on how we feel and in time, what we believe about who we are and the world in which we live. The diagram below shows how each phase drives the next:

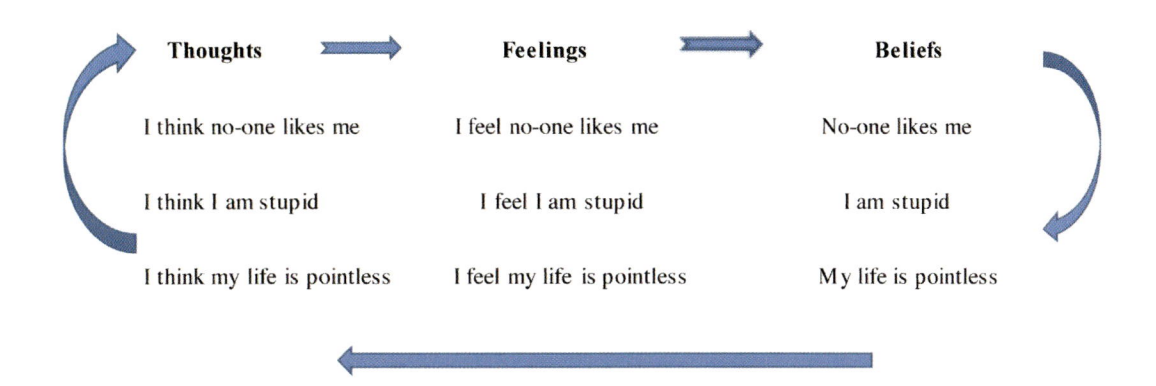

| Thoughts → | Feelings → | Beliefs |
|---|---|---|
| I think no-one likes me | I feel no-one likes me | No-one likes me |
| I think I am stupid | I feel I am stupid | I am stupid |
| I think my life is pointless | I feel my life is pointless | My life is pointless |

What we need to understand here, and we need to help our children recognise this too, is that thoughts are our brain's way of assessing our lives and fundamentally to keep us alive. Our thoughts are mini risk assessments, taking in information to keep going. Yet thoughts are in fact just guesses, they are supposed to come and go. Sometimes thoughts stay around longer than they need to and we can become fused to them, which causes us to spend more time and attention thinking about them and which then activates the thoughts – feelings – beliefs cycle.

Once our emotions have been activated we also function less rationally, logically and even intelligently. In fact, research suggests that we are 30% less intelligent due to our frontal lobes shutting down!

We need to teach our children that our brains might provide us with lots of thoughts but they are not always fact. We need to question our thinking and where necessary, find evidence to help us challenge or support them.

It is also important for us to realise how damaging these negative thoughts can become long term. By overthinking a thought and giving it a lot of time and attention, it can hugely impact on our confidence, our capabilities and how we feel we are coping with life in general. Small things can quickly escalate into much bigger issues. However, our brains are amazing and with insight and action (see diagram in Introduction) we can move things forward and even make significant neurological brain changes in the process.

## *Negative thinking patterns that we can all experience*

When children and young people like Bladen and Tim are flooded with negative thoughts about themselves, this begins to create internal messages about who they believe they are. These irrational thoughts that can deceive them into thinking that what they are feeling is fact. By understanding that we can all do this sometimes, this can make it much easier to not only separate ourselves from the thoughts but more importantly, question them too.

Throughout the story, Bladen and Tim engage in many negative thinking patterns which lead to negative behaviour choices. Some examples are:

### *Personalising*

Sometimes children and young people can become too inward looking and consumed with their life and their world. This intense thinking that everything is about them and that the world revolves around them can become very overwhelming and can lead to them blaming any failings or disasters on themselves. This can lead to children and young people thinking that when something goes wrong, it must be their fault.

The level of personalising can range from a friend being in a bad mood to parents separating. The child will assume that it must be because of something they have done. When engaged in this mindset, children and young people see themselves as a magnet for negative experiences which can therefore, understandably, negatively affect self-esteem.

### *Labelling*

Children and young people can very often feel negatively labelled or judged based on past events. They see themselves as either good or bad. Labels can be created very quickly, dependent on the behaviour choices that have been used. Children and young people are always very good at naming the labels they have gained and the reasons why, but they are also aware that these labels can lead them at times to being targeted for incidents they have not been involved in. This negative labelling can impact on self-esteem; feelings of resentment and, in turn, anger feeds the negative behaviour cycle.

### *Selfishness*

In the story, Bladen struggles to decide which friend to choose to help her to do a job for the teacher. Larry Love-Who-You-Are helps her to understand that it is okay to think about ourselves sometimes. This is not selfish; this is essential for long-term positive self-esteem and well-being. There are in fact three kinds of selfish:

- *Negatively Selfish* - This selfishness is often associated with being mean, unkind and putting our own needs first without any regard to the impact of others. Continued acts of this kind of selfishness can be a sign of low self-esteem, as children and young people feel that they need to get what they can whenever they can, as they feel they are less worthy than others to receive it freely

- *Martyrdom* – This is the polar opposite to negatively selfish. It is when our own needs are not thought about at all and no matter what, we always put others' needs before our own. This can also be a sign of low self-esteem, as children and young people are considering themselves less important than anyone else and are driven by the deep-rooted need for others to like and need them, which validates who they are. It can also develop lots of underlying feelings of resentment and confirmation, feelings that they are not important as no-one else ever appears to give to them what they give to others

- *Positively Selfish* – This sits between negative, selfish and martyrdom. And is thought to be the healthiest for good self-esteem. It is about taking a balanced view of situations and allowing individual needs to be considered in the outcome. By being positively selfish, we reflect on the impact of how others might feel but also justify our own needs gently and assertively

**FEAR *(Face Everything And Recover)***

Many children and young people can struggle to take on new challenges, especially if low self-esteem marries with anxiety. The FEAR concept helps us to develop resilience to new or stressful situations or triggers. In order for positive progression and development, the exposure to the stress needs to be a little uncomfortable and challenging but not too strong as to do more harm. It is about using small steps to nudge towards the desired goal, not about the person being terrified or overwhelmed, as this will reinforce feelings of not coping. The FEAR model can be taught through visualisation, role-play or real life, e.g.:

- Children seeing themselves on an imaginary TV walking into a room full of new people
- Children do the same as above but are in 'the experience'
- Children imagine themselves on TV knowing the people are all lovely and kind
- Children repeat the last stage while in the image
- Children see themselves on TV having fun and laughing with the room full of people. They might be encouraged to put silly clothes on the crowd, develop feelings of familiarity, love or humour
- Repeat the last stage while imagining themselves in that moment
- In real life suggest that children take a note to the office or the next classroom, in order to move forward into reality

It is important to record what goes well at each stage and for children to reflect on two scores:

1. Anticipated fear level 1-10
2. Actual fear level 1-10

This helps children and young people notice positive progress which, over time, will boost self-esteem.

**Top tips to reduce the impact of negative thinking patterns**

- Look out for children and young people who might engage in negative thinking patterns. If they do, listen and help them understand what they are doing
- Empathise – put yourself in their shoes and try to imagine what they are feeling. Never dismiss anything as silly or stupid as that is what they will feel they are
- Set up new thinking scripts. Instead of "I am stupid, I always make mistakes." Change it to "mistakes are good, they mean I am learning."
- Listen out for negative dialogues so that you can help children question and challenge them
- Be realistic with alternative thinking rather than overly positive. Rather than "You are going to love your new school, it will be brilliant and you will make lots of new friends" say "Starting a new school can be a bit scary for everyone, but once you start to settle in and make new friends, you will begin to love it."
- Remember that thoughts are just guesses; let them come and go whenever possible
- Recognise these negative thinking patterns in yourself. The more you understand yourself, what you are doing and why, the better your parental self-esteem will be
- If you use the FEAR method, always make sure the challenge in this process is not disabling (too little challenge = no progress, too much challenge = backwards progress)
- Try to avoid using the terms good and bad for behaviour choices as this can lead children to feeling they are either good or bad. Use right or wrong instead
- Remind children and young people that CBT techniques require repetition and practise:
    - ✓ The problem won't be solved first time
    - ✓ Failures are as important as successes
    - ✓ Failure shows we need to try something else
    - ✓ Success = shows we got it right
    - ✓ Partial success = let's keep trying to improve even more
- Forgive and accept yourself and your mistakes; you are not and don't need to be perfect

- Remember the successes, not just the failures
- Don't set yourself up for failure, be realistic
- Not everything can be solved right now. Sometimes it takes time and consideration

### ***Questions for discussion with children and young people.***

1. Have you ever felt like Bladen and Tim? What negative things do you say to yourself sometimes?

2. What do you say to yourself when you make a mistake? What could you say instead?

3. Do you ever find yourself focussing on things that need to be changed? Learn to let them go. Good self-esteem isn't about being perfect; it's about accepting your faults. Write a list of all the wonderful things that make you you, and your weaknesses. Try to write 5 positive things for every negative thing.

4. Complete this recipe for happiness with things you like (e.g. friends, football, playing in the park, favourite music or films)
    - ✓ 500g of_____
    - ✓ 250g of_____
    - ✓ 100ml of_____
    - ✓ A dash of_____
    - ✓ A pinch of_____

5. As often as you can, do the things you wrote in your recipe for happiness. Why not create other recipes for different emotions and feelings?

## Section 3- How low self-esteem affects behaviour

Our levels of self–esteem very much reflect how much we like and love ourselves. This self-love has a huge impact on what we feel we are capable of, what we believe other people think of us, and also how sensitive we are to rejection, mistakes and difficult life events.

There is a strong connection between how we see ourselves (self-perception), how much we value that idea of ourselves (self-esteem) and the behaviours we present.

- ☺ *Self-perception* is based on what we think about ourselves; how capable we think we are intellectually, physically, athletically, socially emotionally and behaviourally
- ☺ *Self-esteem* is based on our beliefs of our perception of self-linked with how we judge or evaluate it (like or dislike), how we feel about who we are and our sense of self-worth
- ☺ *Behaviour* is driven by success or failure

In almost all cases of children and young people with behavioural issues, self-esteem will play a key role and so needs to be considered and supported before negative behaviour can change. Children and young people need to feel safe, happy and valued in order for positive self-perception and self-image to develop. It is self-esteem which affects how we perceive much of our potential, and how much we apply and make the most of our true abilities.

The foundations of self-esteem include having basic physiological needs met (i.e. food, shelter, clothing), security (feeling safe in our environment), a sense of belonging (love and acceptance from social groups such as family, friends, peers). This concept was devised by Abraham Maslow in 1954 as a developmental hierarchy of needs.

**MASLOW'S MOTIVATION MODEL**

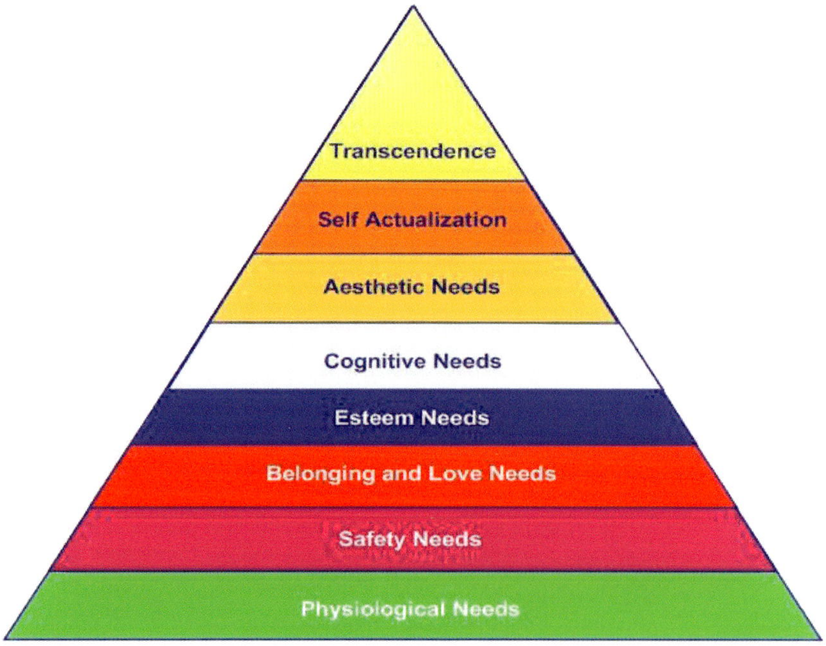
Transcendence
Self Actualization
Aesthetic Needs
Cognitive Needs
Esteem Needs
Belonging and Love Needs
Safety Needs
Physiological Needs

This model shows how important positive self-esteem is in developing our intelligence capabilities (cognitive needs), our ability to recognise beauty in people or the world (aesthetic needs), our drive to improve who we are (self-actualisation needs) and finally our ability to share and teach from our life wisdom and findings (transcendence). It is suggested that needs at each level need to be met in order for us to move on to the next.

Children and young people with low self-esteem often feel that they are not listened to, or that their opinions are not important or considered. Interestingly, this can also be one of the factors that can facilitate low self-esteem in the first place. This can lead to these children being more expressive, louder and offering out 'big' behaviours as a way of saying "notice me, help me." These behaviour choices can also have a negative effect on others and how others react to these children which, in turn, reinforces the vicious cycle of low self-esteem.

Therefore, self-esteem is also an essential component in being able to develop assertively, which underpins our capacity to express feelings, needs and ideas confidently and without aggression (negatively selfish) or obedience (martyrdom).

Adults naturally have role-power over children and young people; low self-esteem can lead to children and young people challenging adults' suggestions, or refusing to reflect or accept responsibility, which again causes further problems. Other negative behaviours can be:

- Withdrawing
- Aggression and dominance
- Boastfulness
- Discomfort with new people
- Difficulty in developing positive relationships
- Problems keeping friends
- Self-criticism
- Avoidance of academic, social situations or challenges
- Struggling to make choices

These behaviours can make childhood a lonely place. Most children and young people with low self-esteem are most often highly sensitive and so not only hurt the easiest, but also struggle to bounce back from ongoing difficult life events. Regardless of the reasons, as parents, carers, professionals and active adults in each child's life, we have a role to play in adding some currency to each child or young person and, in turn, improving their sense of wellbeing and worth.

<u>*Self-esteem, language and behaviour*</u>

As adults, we need to be very careful of the language we use with children, as it very quickly builds up a catalogue that supports the development of who they think they are.

Remember, unkind words are remembered for much longer than kind ones. Here are some helpful things to know:

- ✓ Don't use "I don't care" as children hear that we don't care about them rather than about the issue
- ✓ It is okay to get cross occasionally but only if we bombard them with

praise most of the time
- ✓ Thank children for something done well
- ✓ Give warm body language and smile. Children and young people want our eyes to light up when we see them
- ✓ Praise and be positive as often as possible
- ✓ Remain emotionally available, don't distance or give up
- ✓ Avoid sarcasm and put downs at all costs
- ✓ Label the behaviour not the child, "That wasn't very kind what you said to your brother. You are better than that behaviour" rather than "You are unkind and nasty for what you just said to your brother"
- ✓ Don't make children and young people feel small. They are likely to behave bigger and brasher than they usually feel
- ✓ Try not to correct children in front of others. They will take much more notice if you do it in private
- ✓ Avoid making mistakes feel like sins, as it upsets their values
- ✓ Don't make rash promises, this makes children feel very let down when the promises are not carried through
- ✓ Don't dismiss questions, otherwise children and young people will seek information elsewhere
- ✓ Apologise when necessary. It makes children feel warm towards us
- ✓ Avoid amateur psychology – "you just don't think, you just don't try"
- ✓ Avoid telling children that their fears are silly or not real. They feel very real to the child or young person and they are desperate for you to understand and reassure them
- ✓ Don't dine out on being perfect on flawless, we need to accept our faults too
- ✓ Don't label, "people like you, you're a child"
- ✓ Comparisons are very negative, "your sister never does that, why can't you be like…"
- ✓ Don't exaggerate, "you always/never/can't do anything right"

### ***Questions & tasks for discussion with children and young people.***

1. Think of a time when you felt confident and satisfied with what you had done.
   - What was the situation?
   - What were you saying to yourself at that time (self-talk)?
   - What were you feeling in your body, mind and emotions?
   - What did this occasion teach you?

2. Now think of a time when you felt a loss of confidence or satisfaction with what you had done.
   - What was the situation?
   - What were you saying to yourself at that time (self-talk)?
   - What were you feeling in your body, mind and emotions?
   - What could you do differently next time?

3. Keep a 'feel good' diary. Write down at least five things every day that you are grateful for or what puts a smile on your face. You can use this diary as a positive reminder on difficult days.

4. Answer the following statements as fully as you can:
   - ✓ I like myself because…
   - ✓ People who love me are…
   - ✓ My friends and family like me because…
   - ✓ I know a lot about…
   - ✓ I am good at…
   - ✓ My best qualities are…
   - ✓ Things I like most about my appearance are…
   - ✓ I feel calm when…
   - ✓ Goals for my future are…

5. Remember all the ace things in the list above. Think positive things about yourself to feel positive things about yourself.

**Section 4 – Self-esteem and Emotional Development**

Emotions are an essential part of our lives as they inform us about whether something is right or wrong. As a situation arises, our brains gather all the incoming information about what is happening. This activates "the feeling" centre of the brain from where all the emotions emerge and operate.

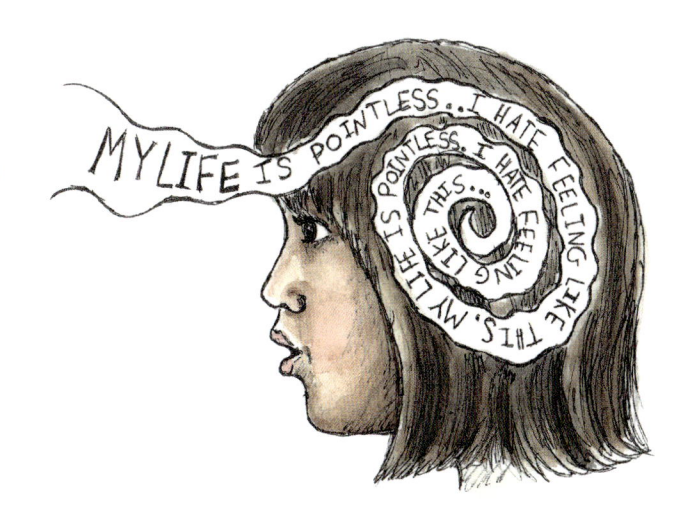

The essential purpose of emotion is to help us to adapt adequately to environmental changes for basic survival.

The quality and extent of emotional responsiveness depends on the value and strength of our core beliefs (mental states) which develop from past experiences.
Emotional development involves many intellectual and social processes including:
- recognising emotions and managing them
- accurate choice-making
- developing care and compassion for ourselves (self-esteem) and others
- coping with difficult situations effectively
- developing and maintaining positive relationships

Research suggests that all animals are born with primary emotions: fear, joy, anger, and surprise. With young children, a lot of these emotions can be seen through automatic responses as possibly the best form of communication - crying!! It is a lot easier to tell if a baby is upset or angry than if it is happy.

Basic emotions are experienced by people globally and each consists of three elements:

- A subjective feeling
- A physiological change
- A visible behaviour

When dealing with emotions, children use social referencing to learn how to react to unfamiliar situations. If a child watches their caregiver saying 'Yuck!' to a piece of fruit, the child will react similarly when presented with a similar situation. Just as parents model behaviours for their children, they also model emotions.

As with most developmental issues, the early years and the infant-caregiver relationship is thought to be where emotional development begins. If we are not aware of what we are feeling or more importantly what to do with that emotion in order to change it for the better, then we will not be as effective in guiding our children's emotional development and resilience.

In Erikson's theory of psychosocial development (1968) below, we can see the developmental stages children need to pass through successfully in order to make progress as typically developing children.

| Stage | Basic Conflict | Important Events | Outcome |
|---|---|---|---|
| **Infancy (birth to 18 months)** | Trust vs. Mistrust | Feeding | Children develop a sense of trust when caregivers provide reliability, care and affection. A lack of this will lead to mistrust. |
| **Early Childhood (2 to 3 years)** | Autonomy vs. Shame and Doubt | Toilet Training | Children need to develop a sense of personal control over physical skills and a sense of independence. Success leads to feelings of autonomy, failure results in feelings of shame and doubt. |
| **Preschool (3 to 5 years)** | Initiative vs. Guilt | Exploration | Children need to begin asserting control and power over the environment. Success in this stage leads to a sense of purpose. Children who try to exert too much power experience disapproval, resulting in a sense of guilt. |
| **School Age (6 to 11 years**_ | Industry vs. Inferiority | School | Children need to cope with new socail and academic demands. Success leads to a sense of competence, while failure results in feelings of inferiority. |
| **Adolescence (12 to 18 years)** | Identity vs. Role Confusion | Social Relationships | Teens need to develop a sense of self and personal identity. Success leads to an ability to stay true to yourself, while failure leads to role confusion and a weak sense of self. |
| **Young Adulthood (19 to 40 years)** | Intimacy vs. Isolation | Relationships | Young adults need to form intimate, loving relationships with other people. Success leads to strong relationships, while failure results in loneliness and isolation. |

From the above chart, we can see how our engagement with our children at each stage might predict different emotional and behavioural characteristics including levels of self-esteem. A child who does not receive the correct affirmations or understanding about who they are and what they feel during the early years could become emotionally hindered and struggle to move through the stages naturally. This could have a huge impact on their development of positive self-esteem.

As the active adults in our children's lives, it is important that we learn to model, name and claim the feelings we are feeling, and share this with our children. Our brains need us to recognise our emotions as they tell us vital information. If we choose to ignore our negative emotional communication, our brains will turn the volume up on those feelings until the emotion becomes unbearable and we need to stop to do something about it. At this stage our brains virtually breathe a sigh of relief, as if to say, at last, you have noticed something important and now you can action it.

In the development of emotional understanding and particularly for children who are experiencing low self-esteem, trying new things and refusing to do things that adults know that they can do, can often happen due to an underlying fear of getting things wrong or failing. Failure phobia is a way of children not having to confirm to themselves or others that they are not capable, whether this is reality or not.

Some children refuse to maintain control, especially if anxiety plays a part. However, anxious children and young people need to be encouraged to face up to difficult situations so that they feel empowered and can also internalise beliefs that they are capable and that they can.

In this situation, it is important for adults to be as understanding as possible and adjust our language and perspective in order to maintain levels of calm and patience. It is essential however that we try to grasp what the child is gaining from this avoidant behaviour so that we know what they need from us to move it forward.

**Top tips to support healthy emotional development**
- Encourage your children with love, guidance, patience, understanding and firm boundaries when needed
- Overdose them with positive affirmations that allow them to be who they are
- Help your children to name and claim emotions and feelings
- Try to use do's rather than don'ts
- Try to stop being self-critical with yourself, as this models low-self-esteem in your

children

- Use real life stories and experiences from your life to help children learn about emotional situations as this teaches them about the realities of life, that we can and do cope. This is more likely to activate positive self-talk
- Be flexible when children are refusing. Sometimes we demand they do homework, etc. when we think they should do it. A little bit of co-operation from us is more likely to encourage them to do what is required
- Don't be a master of learned incompetence. Children and young people will naturally stall, delay or refuse if they think you will eventually do it for them
- Don't help too much. Children need to struggle a bit in order to learn and develop a stronger sense of self. Nevertheless, the trick is to know when to hold back and when to help if a task is truly beyond their ability
- Give children some responsibility. They need to learn that they can. This also fosters independence, emotional maturity and continued learning
- If you feel concerned about your child's self-esteem or emotional development and resilience, check in with school and get their perspective in order to see a more complete picture

**Section 5 – Your role in supporting children with low-self-esteem**

As a parent, carer or teacher, our role is dominated by the needs of our children. However, we can unconsciously forget the importance of nurturing positive self-esteem especially during times of difficult behaviours.

It is suggested that we actually show the greatest love to our children when they are being challenged rather than when they are making positive choices. It is easy to praise and support children and young people when things are going well but a different, and perhaps more damaging message, can be received when things are not going quite so well. Some important guidelines for us to consider are:

- ✓ Catch your child making the right choices
- ✓ Positively reinforce the positive behaviours with lots of encouraging praise and feedback
- ✓ Instead of using direct praises, e.g. "That is good", use more specific praise, e.g. "I really like how you have used those colours in your picture". Children with low self-esteem will reject praise that is saying they are good as they don't feel good. If you use more subjective praise they are more likely to accept it
- ✓ Celebrate achievements with family and friends and let them see that you are proud of them whenever possible
- ✓ Find as many opportunities to tell them that they are brilliant, e.g. saying please and thank you, following instructions, being kind, helping, learning a new skill, telling the truth, doing their best, reading at home
- ✓ If you aren't happy about a situation, disapprove the behaviour not the child, e.g. "I don't like that behaviour, it makes me feel..."

- ✓ Remember for the development of positive self-esteem we need more positives than negatives (5:1) so check your ratio regularly
- ✓ Seek out your child's opinion and show that you value their input
- ✓ Spend quality time together and use this as a reward for life choices
- ✓ Recognise and encourage positive characteristics, e.g. effort, bravery, strength, creativity, honesty, humour, organisation, good manners, and talent
- ✓ Use the 5 A's in your relationship with children and young people in order to raise self-esteem:

|  | What you are saying | What the child hears |
|---|---|---|
| Affection | I like/love you | I am loved/cared for |
| Appreciate | Thank you for… | I am noticed |
| Accept | You are okay | I am okay |
| Affirm | I know lots of brilliant things about you | I am special and worthwhile |
| Attention | I see you | I am important |

- ✓ Share your experiences of the day, positive and negative
- ✓ Keep conversations open and supportive
- ✓ Apologise when necessary; it will make children feel surprisingly warm towards you
- ✓ Use 'winning' dialogue, e.g. "Well done", "You can do it", "I have confidence in you", "I am sure you can handle it", "Mistakes are okay"
- ✓ Avoid being judgmental and intolerant of the views of others
- ✓ Remember children and young people are growing up quickly, try and keep pace
- ✓ Extend responsibilities as they mature, developing and increasing their levels of trust and judgement in different situations

Things to avoid saying/doing at all costs:
- ✗ *"What's wrong with you?"* This phrase fosters feelings of shame and embarrassment and lays the issue solely with the child. Difficult situations are a complex mix of expectations, mood, experiences and perceptions

- *"You had better do that or else"* This statement is instigating feelings of fear and if our children are scared of us, then they will not come to us with their emotional needs. It also models intimidation and aggression as a form of getting what we want and your little children will one day be much bigger young people who could then start using it on you
- *"You're driving me mad"* This sentence induces deep feelings of guilt. It also teaches children that they can be responsible for creating negative feelings in others which will most definitely develop feelings of low self-esteem
- Don't make children feel smaller than they are, otherwise they are likely to behave stupidly big
- Try not to correct them in front of other people. Children and young people will take much more notice if you talk to them quietly in private
- Don't make big promises. Children and young people will feel badly let down when promises are broken
- Try not to question their honesty too much, as it can frighten children and young people into telling lies
- Don't put them off when asking questions. They want to learn from you, otherwise they will stop asking and try and find answers from others

## Summary

This book has aimed to provide you with some of the important emotional and behavioural theories to help you gain a greater understanding of the psychology of self-esteem. The more emotionally aware we are about emotions, the greater support we can provide to children and young people who are struggling to understand very intense negative feelings about themselves or about life.

All children and young people will experience negative life events which could impact on self-esteem. Life is tough at times, but we need to help our children to develop skills, in order to deal with what life brings and move difficult feelings on. We need to accept emotions before we can even think about regulating them. By helping our children to develop a strong sense of who they are and what they are feeling, they can begin to develop in ways that are not only assertive, responsible and emotionally intelligent, but also that develop a worthy sense of well-being and resilience across the lifespan for themselves and their future generations.

**Self-esteem - Summary Checklist – little things that can help in a big way!**

- Start as young as possible with the tips in this book. It is easier to create a child's positive self-esteem than it is to improve it
- Remember that improving the value of a young person takes time
- *Every smile, positive comment, engaging conversation, listening if they are upset, comforting gesture if you know they seem unhappy, asking "How are you today?", or a second of forgiveness even if the last hour was a nightmare, gives children and young people a currency which fosters feelings of worth

- Accept your weaknesses. We are all flawed and all have faults. Positive self-esteem isn't about being perfect, it is about liking ourselves wholeheartedly – warts and all!

- We have all felt saddened when a child or young person shows total refusal to stop a behaviour when asked but then someone else can ask and they do it straight away! The words exchanged are about 5% of the action; the quality of interactions prior to this event is the other 95%. A child who feels you understand and care will not want to let you down as you make them feel different Make them feel okay and that means the world

- Encourage decision making, choices and opinions. Self-esteem becomes more established when we feel confident in making the right choices relatively quickly. By giving our children these opportunities, they build a bank of confidence-building tools in their self-esteem kit

- Praise must be specific, saying "That is good" does not register as they do not usually feel good at or about anything. By being specific, e.g. "I really like the way that you have……", the child or young person is less likely to reject this praise or you and develop neurological hooks to add further praise into

- Help children and young people acknowledge their achievements. Keep a log to remind them on difficult days

- Strive to be a better parent, carer, teacher but be realistic. It won't all happen at once so set small, realistic targets and measure your successes

- Remember the 80:20 rule. Like yourself as much as you can for most of the time (80%). This sets a positive level of well-being and helps to buffer us on more difficult days

- Be supportive in conflict. Listen non-judgementally even if there is a possibility that it is their fault. Show them that you are listening and that you understand their point of view. When children know that they have a parent to lean on and who loves and accepts them no matter what, this impacts hugely on their development of positive self-esteem

- Teach your children to reflect on the past and learn from it but don't get overwhelmed with regret. Once the lesson has been learned, let it go and move on

- Bite your lip sometimes! If you need to criticise, do it with a concerned rather than aggressive tone. If you do get cross, apologise afterwards and explain why you felt like you did
- Try it and see. Set yourself personal challenges to change how you engage with your child or young person, even if you action it at the beginning, the results will make it worthwhile for you time after time. Win win!

If you and your child have enjoyed The Blinks – Self-esteem (book 3 in this series) then look out for the first and second books, The Blinks– Worry and The Blinks - Anger, readily available online. Also, keep an eye out for the fourth book in the series, The Blinks – Sadness, due for release in 2017.

To get in touch on social media, please go to:
Facebook - /Theblinksbooks
Twitter - @BlinksThe

## OTHER TITLES IN THE SERIES

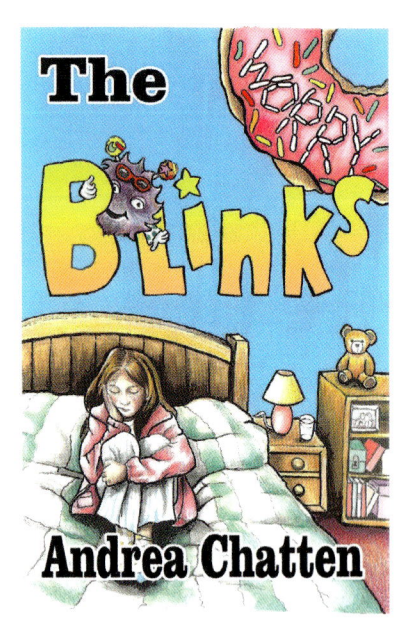

'The Blinks – Worry' is the first novel in the Blinks series of books. The first book in the series is to help all children and young people understand how worry and anxiety present. It is written as a fiction book with many messages and guidance woven into the stories about Amanda and her friends.

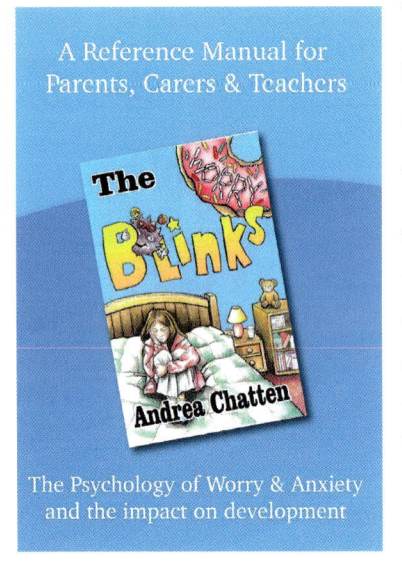

The Blinks books were created to help children, young people, and their families, understand emotional and behavioural issues. More so, it was to provide strategies and techniques to help manage and change the intensity and duration of problematic behaviours over time.

This supportive booklet provides a deeper understanding of the psychology of worrying and how it can impact on other developmental issues including self-esteem and emotions. It also provides lots of 'top tips' on what works best for children and young people whilst growing up and some activity questions that can be used as a starting point to initiate emotive dialogue or discussion with children.

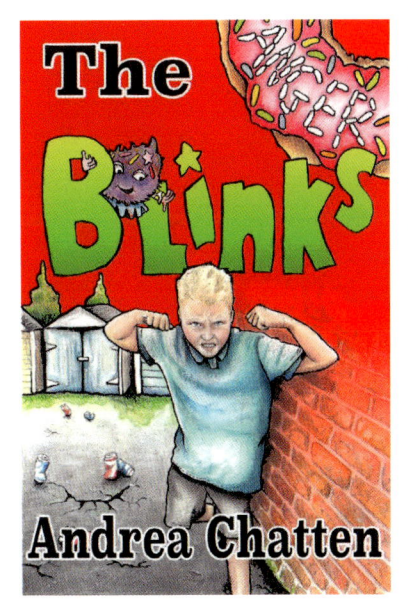

'The Blinks – Anger' is the second novel in the Blinks series of books. This book is to help all children and young people understand the strong emotion of anger and what to do with it to remain in charge. Robbie's life has never been great, but the events over the last few years have slowly made him more and more unhappy and angry. One day it all gets too much, and his anger erupts!

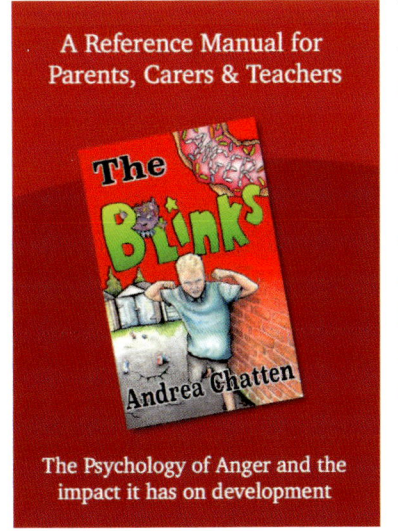

This supportive booklet accompanies the book 'The Blinks – Anger' written specifically for older children and those in their early teens.

It provides a deeper understanding of the psychology of anger for parents, carers and teachers, and how anger can impact on other developmental issues and all other emotions. It also provides lots of 'top tips' on what works best for children and young people whilst growing up and some activity questions that can be used as a starting point to initiate emotive dialogue or discussion with children.

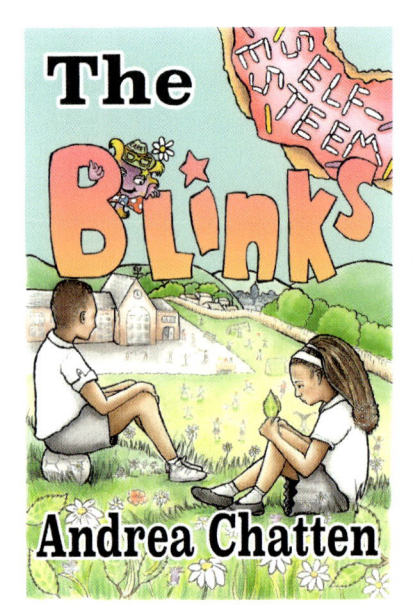

Bladen and Tim are twins who have spent many years being unkind to each other. This has not helped them develop very positive feelings about themselves. Their low self-esteem has affected their confidence, friendships, who they believe they are and their happiness.

Things have been difficult for many years, but then the unthinkable happens and Bladen and Tim think that it is their fault. This makes them like themselves even less. Larry Love-Who-You-Are recognises this difficult situation and works hard to help the twins and himself overcome some very personal challenges.

TO PURCHASE ANY OF THE ABOVE BOOKS IN THE SERIES GO TO:

www.theblinks.co.uk

Also available in print and on Amazon and as a Kindle.